A COMPACT HISTORY OF IRELAND

941
.5

SARAH HEALY

MERCIER PRESS

CONTENTS

A Chronology of Irish History   7

1   The Course of Irish History   13

2   *Gael, Gall* and *Gall-Gaelach*   36

3   Fighting Back   44

4   The Black North   69

5   Decline and Revival   81

Select Bibliography   95

CONTENTS

1. A Chronology of Brief History
2. The Great Wild History
3. Lord God and God's World
4. Fighting Back
5. The Black North
6. Decline and Revival
    Select Bibliography

A CHRONOLOGY OF IRISH HISTORY

30000BC	Ireland's topography established
7000–6500BC	Human habitation at Mount Sandel, near Coleraine, County Derry
2500BC	Building of passage graves, notably Newgrange
680BC	Building of the enclosure at Emain Macha, near Armagh City
AD1–500	Ireland covered with crannogs, hill-forts and raths
77–84	Roman invasion considered but finally rejected by Agricola (40–93)
200	Conn Céd-cathach ('hundred battles') establishes high-kingship at Tara
300–450	Irish raids on Roman Britain
432	Traditional date of the coming of Patrick to Ireland
c. 500–600	Establishment of monasticism as the characteristic feature of the Celtic Church
563	Colum Cille establishes a monastery on Iona
575	Convention at Druim-Cett
590	Columbanus begins his mission to Burgundy
664	Synod of Whitby finds against the Celtic Church
795	First Viking raids
c. 841	Dublin established as permanent Scandinavian colony
975–1014	Brian Boru of Dál Cais (County Clare) *Imperator Scottorum* (King of Ireland)

1014	Battle of Clontarf, death of Brian and final defeat of Scandinavian Irish
1132–1148	Reform of Irish Church by St Malachy
1155	Bull *Laudabiliter* granted to Henry II of England by Pope Adrian IV
1169	Coming of the Anglo-Normans
1170	Landing of Strongbow
1171	Henry II lands to establish the English presence
1315	Invasion of Edward Bruce
1367	Statutes of Kilkenny
1395	Submission of all but northern chieftains to Richard II
1478–1513	Rule of Garret Mór Fitzgerald
1492	Poynings Law makes Dublin parliament subservient to that in London
1541	Henry VIII proclaimed king of Ireland
1557–8	Establishment of King's and Queen's Counties in the lands of Offaly and Laois
1586	Plantation of Munster
1593–1603	Nine Years' War between O'Neill and his allies and the English forces
1601	O'Neill's defeat at Kinsale
1607	'Flight of the Earls'
1608–10	Plantation of Ulster
1641	Native Irish rebellion
1642	Owen Roe O'Neill takes command of the forces of the Irish Confederacy
1646	Victory for Owen Roe at Benburb
1649	Death (by poisoning?) of Owen Roe and Cromwellian massacres at Drogheda and Wexford
1653	Forfeiture of Irish lands
1660	Restoration of Charles II
1681	Execution of St Oliver Plunkett
1687	Tyrconnell made lord deputy by James II
1689	Relief of the beseiged anti-Jacobites in Derry
1690	Battle of the Boyne; departure of James II
1691	(Soon to be broken) Treaty of Limerick

	signed
1695	Penal laws against Catholics
1704	Further penal laws (in Queen Anne's reign)
1778	Formation of the Irish Volunteers
1782	Dungannon convention of the Volunteers and proclamation of legislative independence
1791	Foundation of United Irishmen in Belfast
1795	'Battle of the Diamond' at Loughgall, County Armagh and establishment of the Orange Order
1798	Rebellion in Antrim, Down, Wexford and Mayo
1800	Act of Union
1829	Catholic Emancipation
1831–2	Tithe War
1842	Charles Gavan Duffy, co-founder with Thomas Davis of the Young Ireland Movement becomes editor of the *Nation*
1845–8	Famine caused by potato blight; population diminished by two million due to death and emigration
1867	Unsuccessful Fenian rising
1869	Gladstone disestablishes the Church of Ireland
1877	Parnell assumes leadership of Irish Parliamentary Party, the more effective by reason of the obstructive tactics of his lieutenant, J. G. Biggar
1879	Davitt founds the Land League
1890	Fall of Parnell and serious schism in the Irish party
1892	Gladstone's Second Home Rule Bill defeated
1893	Foundation of the Gaelic League
1910	Carson becomes leader of Irish unionists
1912	Solemn League and Covenant against Home Rule signed by 218,000 Protestants
1913	Foundation of the Irish Citizen Army, UVF and (in response) Irish Volunteers

1914	Curragh 'mutiny', UVF gun-running, outbreak of Great War (and agreed postponement of terms of Third Home Rule Bill)
1916	Easter Rising; unionists agree to a partitioned Ulster
1919–21	Anglo-Irish War
1920	Ulster partitioned under Government of Ireland Act
1921	Anglo-Irish Treaty
1922	Outbreak of Civil War (ceases in 1923); Special Powers Act (NI)
1926	Foundation of Fianna Fáil by de Valera
1932	Fianna Fáil government; tariff 'war' with Britain (agreement in 1938)
1939	Éire declares its neutrality at outbreak of war
1948	Declaration of republic by Taoiseach Costello; N. Ireland shares in benefits of Britain's 'welfare state'
1951	'Mother and child scheme' controversy damages coalition government
1965	Meeting between Terence O'Neill and Sean Lemass, opposition by Ian Paisley
1968	Police clash with Northern Ireland Civil Rights Association march in Derry followed by severe rioting
1969	British army called in to prevent civil strife in Derry and (after anti-Catholic attacks) Belfast
1970	Start of Provisional IRA's campaign (lasts with several ceasefires until 1998)
1972	'Bloody Sunday' (Derry) fourteen anti-Internment demonstrators killed by British paratroopers; Stormont prorogued
1974	Power-sharing executive brought down by Ulster Workers Council strike
1981	Ten hunger-strikers die in 'special category' campaign
1985	Anglo-Irish Agreement

1988	Talks between John Hume of the SDLP and Gerry Adams of Sinn Féin
1994	IRA ceasefire (broken February 1996)
1995	Divorce referendum passed by narrow majority
1998	Good Friday Agreement

1

THE COURSE OF IRISH HISTORY

One of the venerable books of Ireland the *Lebor Gabála* (Book of Taking), compiled in the eleventh century, describes the history of Ireland from the Creation of the world to the time of its compilation. The 'takings' were done by many waves of invaders, including those of Cesair, the granddaughter of Noah, Partholón, Nemed, the Fir Bolg (Men of Bags), the Tuatha Dé Danann (the Celtic pantheon) and the Gaels, called here the Milesians. Though the accounts of the earliest invasions are mythologised, they were undoubtedly based upon tradition and folk memory and when the magic is peeled away the book does establish the central authentic fact of at least the first two thousand years of Irish history. The island of Ireland was subject to a series of, if not actually

13

invasions in the military sense, then immigrations or 'conquests' by peaceful means. All the peoples who arrived in this manner were eventually assimilated until the establishment of the Anglo-Norman colony in the years AD 1169–1333.

The earliest settlers were probably nomadic and may have crossed by the land bridges that were to disappear after the melting of 100,000 years of ice. Even when these causeways were swept away – the most notable was that which linked the basalt formations of the Giant's Causeway in Antrim and Fingal's Cave in Staffa in the Inner Hebrides – the journeys across the narrow sea from Kintyre to north Antrim, Galloway to Down, Anglesey to Dublin or Rosslare to Fishguard were short if not always calm. Farmers followed hunters and by the beginning of the Christian era the country was Celtic. The island was kept temperate by the Gulf Stream and the frequent rain made certain an abundant supply of grass for the cattle which served many purposes – as suppliers of food, clothing and building material and currency. With the increase in temperatures that came with the end of the Ice Age, the country had become covered with deep woods; these, along with the boggy interior, made communications difficult. The easiest routes were by the rivers, which made journeys into the interior relatively simple, and the Shannon, Foyle, Bann, Lagan, Slaney, Barrow, Nore, Suir, Blackwater and Lee, taken with the sea loughs, Foyle, Swilly, Donegal Bay, Clew Bay, Galway Bay, Shannon Estuary, the harbours of Cork, Waterford and Wexford, Dublin Bay, Carlingford and Belfast Loughs provided waterways that essentially covered the country. (These waterways made the country more vulnerable to the attacks of the Vikings who came in the eighth century first as marauders but stayed as farmers, merchants and town-builders.)

The Celts had first appeared in central Europe *c.*1200BC, but were pushed to the western fringes of the continent by the Romans and by the Germanic tribes. (The Romans in time conquered England, Wales and southern Scotland but never got around to carrying out their intention of invading the country they called Hibernia – a pun on their words for 'wintry'/ *hibernus* – and the inhabitants *Iverni*.) Those

Celts who settled in Ireland had by the time of the coming of Christianity a highly developed oral language and a respect for their forebears' mighty deeds that amounted almost to worship. Christianity was brought originally in the aftermath of trade and formally by missionaries, notably Patrick, who lived in the fifth century and according to tradition came to Ireland in 432. The Christianising of the Celts was relatively bloodless and many of the learned class, the druids, retained their special cultural and intellectual position in the new Christian society.

As the Church in Ireland developed in the sixth and seventh century, it took on a monastic rather than an episcopal structure. The tradition of living in monastic communities had come from Egypt through Gaul and Britain, and in a remarkably short time Ireland was covered with monastic establishments. These in time formed the nuclei of settlements in a country not noted for towns. They were centres of learning as well as religious practice. The larger monasteries were associated with the land divisions known as *tuatha*. In the seventh century, the period of the first flowering of Irish monasticism, there were about two hundred of these independent entities, ruled by a king (*rí*) whose main roles comprised leader in battle, president of the *oenach* (assembly) and the object of quasi-religious respect. *Tuatha* were usually part of overgroups which in turn were taken to be members of major confederations known as the 'Five Fifths of Ireland', eventually reconstituted as the four provinces (still in Irish called *cúigí* or 'fifths') known as Ulster, Munster, Leinster and Connacht. The largest *oenach* was held yearly at Tara in County Meath, presided over by a high-king (*ard rí*).

The monastic settlement provided the *tuath* with a *de facto* intellectual, social and administrative centre, its stockaded perimeters containing the prison, hospital, marketplace and church, with the abbot the spiritual equivalent of the *rí*. The ecclesiastical structure, however, did nothing to prevent the internecine wars that were such a feature of Irish society and though the island was the centre of great learning and art, and the source of the reChristianising of northern Europe, the nearest it came to being a united country was briefly under the rule of

Brian Boru who died in 1014 at the end of the predominance of the Vikings. Saints there were in plenty and scholars as well, and warriors of noted ferocity in individual battles, but the country could never unite effectively to repel any invader.

This did not matter as long as the incomers could be assimilated. The Vikings eventually settled down to create Ireland's first towns and seaports and teach the Irish commerce, but their raids and irruptions for more than two hundred years did much damage materially and psychologically. By the time of their quiescence, the golden age of Irish monasticism was over and though the scholarship and skill of the artificers was maintained, the Church was in sore need of reform. The main trouble was secularisation, a virtual inevitability in a country that so honoured hereditary rights. Reform came mainly through St Malachy (?1094–1148), the Archbishop of Armagh, his work reflecting the reorganisation of the Church in Europe during the eleventh and twelfth centuries and its virtual independence from secular overlords. Bishops replaced abbots as ecclesiastical rulers, their dioceses corresponding to the *tuath*-clusters of earlier times. The European system of monasticism supplanted that of the old Celtic Church, Malachy himself bringing to Mellifont the first Cistercians to establish a house in Ireland.

One effect of the changes was largely to laicise the intellectual and aesthetic life of the country; another was to provide the Anglo-Normans with a religious reason for placating the 'rude and ignorant' Irish. Henry II of England (1133–89), not a name that springs to mind as a model of piety, was granted Ireland by the only English pope, Adrian IV (1100–59) by the bull *Laudabiliter* (1155). Ireland, especially in its disunited state, was always likely prey for the unruly Anglo-Norman lords and, in the person of the since-execrated Dermot MacMurrough of Leinster, was only too happy to connive in her own despoilment. His amorous involvements and territorial ambitions led to enmity with Rory O Conor, the high-king, and an invitation to the 'Franks' to intervene on his behalf.

When Henry II saw that Richard de Clare ('Strongbow', as he was known) and his party seemed to have profited from their Irish ad-

venture in 1169 he came in person and established the *Gall*, as the largely inattentive Gaels called the foreigners, in Ireland. Three-quarters of the land was in English hands by 1280. Although over the next 250 years the regions where the foreigners held sway were to shrink to the lands of Dublin, Meath and parts of Louth and Kildare, the region known as the Pale – the word coming from the Latin *palus* (stake) by which the boundary of the territories should be marked – the Gall stayed, professing allegiance to the English crown. Though the lords of Ulster and north Connacht soon dismissed the foreigners from their territories and most of the Gall became 'more Irish than the Irish themselves', the loyal English still held to their prosperous enclosure. It was this fatal fealty of a territory, 'scarcely thirty miles in length and twenty in width' that created the Irish Question that has affected so grievously the distressful country since the day in 1541 when Henry VIII declared himself King of Ireland.

Henry's break from Rome and the outlawing of Catholicism made a grave situation worse.

Elizabeth I, who acceded in 1558, would have preferred acquiescence to pacification but her Tudor generals could always persuade her to extreme measures especially by playing upon her fear that the forces of European monarchs in the guise of counter-Reformationists could use Catholic Ireland as a backdoor means of attacking England. Her hope that the chief of the Irish leaders, Hugh O'Neill (*c.*1550–1616) of Tír Eoghain who had been educated in England might lead a peaceful Ireland was dashed when his true intentions became clear. To the 'news from Ireland' which had already included savagely suppressed risings in Leinster and Munster, he addeed the Nine Years' War (1593–1603) which ended with the final defeat of Gaelic Ireland at Kinsale. His attempt to find help from Philip III by leaving for Spain with the lords of Tír Chonaill and Fermanagh in 1607, a gamble known with some justice as the 'Flight of the Earls', misfired and the country was left open for the final effective colonisation.

The seventeenth century saw not only the confiscation of most of the land of Ireland but also the suppression of the native population.

The formal plantation of six counties of Ulster with the addition of the 'unofficially' planted Antrim and Down rooted in a loyal and adamantly alien population of Presbyterian lowland Scots and Anglican English in Ulster. The eventual success of Cromwell's campaigns in 1649–50 and the defeat of the Jacobites by the army of William III in 1690 left Catholic Ireland without an aristocracy or leadership and in possession of only 14 per cent of the land. The debasement of the native population through most of the eighteenth century was intensified by penal laws which were intended to deprive Catholics of all civil and political rights. Catholics were forbidden to practise their religion, could not acquire land nor educate their children at home or abroad. Many of the professions were closed to them and their permitted possessions might not rise above a fixed level. Many of the residual Catholic landowners conformed to the Church of Ireland in order to preserve their properties. In fact, the Catholic manufacturing and mercantile classes were not specifically penalised though they suffered from the other disabilities. The application of the full rigour of the laws varied from place to place and by 1720, in spite of the Bishops Banishment Act (1697), priests and bishops were allowed in most areas to operate discreetly without much interference. No general conversion of Catholics to Protestantism was really desired by the authorities; the aim of the penal laws was to make the Catholics impoverished and powerless, especially by denying them ownership of land.

By the end of the eighteenth century, with the growth of enlightenment ideas, many of the formal disabilities of Catholics were removed by a series of relief acts. The involvement of the regular forces of the British army in the American War of Independence (1775–83) (the American side was strongly supported by mainly Presbyterian immigrants from Ireland), had led to the formation of a force of Protestant Volunteers in 1778–9, ostensibly to guard the country against invasion. The movement led eventually to the repeal of the acts which deprived Ireland of legislative independence and in 1782 a modicum of freedom was obtained for a Dublin parliament. The revolution in France encouraged a limited Jacobinism especially among the Presbyterian merchant class in Belfast who called themselves the United Irishmen, and a shortlived rising in 1798 was put down with great savagery by the regular army aided by a volunteer yeomanry almost entirely Anglican Protestant and in the North largely made up of members of the sectarian Orange Order, which had been instituted in 1795. It was the fear of further unrest, including the belief that the Dublin parliament might opt for full independence from Britain, that led Pitt to force through the Act of Union in 1800, by means of wholesale bribery and unkept promises to Catholics.

The new century was to see the rise of Irish democracy. The last legal disability of Catholics was removed when Catholic Emancipation granted property holders the vote in 1829 – a concession made grudgingly after the successful constitutional campaign of Daniel O'Connell, the Liberator (1775–1847). His continuing agitation for the repeal of the Union was overtaken by the Great Famine of 1845–9 when the potato crop, the staple of three million people, failed in three years out of four. The result was a drop in population of nearly two

million caused by death from starvation and
fever, and mass emigration. The population of
the country had fallen from 8 to 6.5 million by
1851 and to 4.4 million by 1911. The trauma
of peasant hunger and destitution lasted for
many decades, especially since the landlords,
notably the most rapacious in Europe and by
now including some Irish Catholics among
their numbers, increased the pace of evictions of
tenants who had no legal standing, so that
between 1846 and 1853 at least 250,000 were
deprived of their miserable homes.

Of all the wrongs perceived with considerable
justice to have been inflicted by Britain on her
despised island the Great Famine of the 1840s
continues to rank as the most infamous, and all
the special pleading of economic theory and
enshrined inertia have done nothing to mitigate
the charge. Yet in its gruesome way it made the
country a better proposition economically. Its
horrors led Isaac Butt (1813–79) and others to
seek a constitutional solution to Ireland's prob-
lems since the Union was clearly not a success.
The last thirty years of the nineteenth century
were marked by rapid improvements of peasant

and farmer conditions forced by the successful activities of the Land League (1879–82). A number of Land Acts from 1880 to 1903 effectively restored a large portion of rural territory to peasant proprietors. With more general franchise the Irish Parliamentary Party led by Charles Stewart Parnell (1846–91), himself a landlord's son, were often able to hold the balance of power in Westminster and by judicious alliance with Gladstone (1808–98) and his Liberals they created hope for the ideal of at least a limited form of Home Rule.

The home of unionism was the Protestant and relatively prosperous north-east of Ireland, and the liberal aspirations of the United Irishmen of 1798 were largely forgotten in the growth of the artificially fostered industrial city of Belfast. Famine and land agitation alike had considerably less effect in east Ulster, where there were far fewer subsistence farmers and the system of tenure was more equitable. The Protestant majority needed Catholic labourers and, while they could not prevent suffrage, used all local means to prevent its being effective. Catholics were tolerated in the region, though subject to

occasional sectarian violence from the re-estab-
lished Orange Order. The Protestant population
of Ulster, especially in Antrim, Down, Armagh
and north Derry (including the industrial city
of Derry), were too prosperous to heed any voice
of liberalisation.

They were proof too against the siren voice
of armed rising, being scarcely conscious of the
short-lived rebellions of the Young Ireland
Movement (1848) or of Fenianism (1867), which
were to act as a kind of low-key counterpoint
to constitutionalism. The physical force tradition
was awaiting its moment in the new century. All
Gladstone's attempts at introducing Home Rule
legislation were bitterly resisted in parliament
by a Conservative-Unionist alliance, the playing,
as Lord Randolph Churchill (1849–94) put it,
of the 'Orange card', and by effectively organised
riotous protest in the streets of Belfast, Porta-
down and Derry. The fall of Parnell, the disarray
of the Irish party and a number of Tory
governments postponed the question until 1911
when the nationalist MPs led by John Redmond
(1856–1918) again held the balance of power in
Westminster and Asquith (1852–1928) agreed

to a far from radical Home Rule provision. The response from the Ulster unionists, now led by Edward Carson (1854–1935) and James Craig (1871–1940) was the mass signing of the Solemn League and Covenant, the formation of the Ulster Volunteer Force, threats of mutiny from Irish officers in the British Army and gun-running.

The political vacuum left by the fall of Parnell had been filled by a vigorous renaissance of Irish identity mediated in literature, national games, music and dancing, and, under the auspices of the Gaelic League, an enthusiastic move for the restoration of the Irish language. (Irish as a literary language had not survived the seventeenth-century loss of the Gaelic aristo-cracy, the patrons of the poets, and the Great Famine and consequent emigration had seriously diminished the monoglot population who spoke a lively, if dialectic, vernacular.) The move to restore Irish was implicitly revolutionary and became explicitly so under the leadership of Patrick Pearse (1879–1916) and Eoin MacNeill (1867–1945). The latter had formed the Irish Volunteers in 1913 as an answer to the UVF and continued to train its members after the outbreak of the Great War in 1914, when by general agreement the implementation of the Home Rule Bill's provisions was postponed until the end of hostilities. MacNeill saw it as a guarantee of independence, having no great hopes of Asquith's resolution against intransigent unionism nor of Redmond's political power, but he was adamantly against the Irish Republican Brotherhood's (IRB) Easter Rising in 1916, which was essentially old Fenianism reborn.

The rebellion of Easter Week 1916 was a watershed. The drawn-out execution of sixteen of the leaders including Pearse by the military governor General Maxwell (1859–1929) caused a surge of support for further armed struggle to infuse the hitherto largely unsympathetic nationalist population, thousands of whom had close relatives fighting in the Great War – though, unlike the UVF, these 'Home Rulers' were not allowed to form their own regiment. The postwar general election showed a massive support for Sinn Féin as the new militant party called themselves and a War of Independence broke out in January 1919. Characterised by intermittent and localised guerrilla warfare from the IRA, as the Irish Volunteers now called themselves, and savage reprisals by newly formed British forces – Black and Tans and Auxiliaries, – the war caused considerable embarrassment to Britain and a truce in July 1921 ended hostilities.

Negotiations in London ended with the signing of an Anglo-Irish Treay in December 1921 that resulted in a measure of freedom – in the words of one of the chief negotiators, Michael Collins (1890–1922), 'the freedom to achieve freedom', but the cessation of hostilities revealed serious factionalism among the Republican forces. The country in a sense *drifted* towards civil war, which was as much a product of its confused state after the Anglo-Irish War as of disagreement about the terms of the treaty, which had the general support of the people. Eamon de Valera (1882–1975), the senior survivor of the Easter Rising, had avoided the main treaty sessions and though associated with the anti-Treatyites did what he could to bring the often brutal violence to an end. The Civil War lasted from June 1922 until a cessation of fighting called by Frank Aiken (1898–1983), after the death of the intransigent Republican leader Liam Lynch (1890–1923) in April 1923.

The British government had established the statelet of Northern Ireland by the Government of Ireland Act of 1920. Saorstát Éireann, comprising the twenty-six counties that had not been partitioned off, did after many economic and political difficulties achieve a large measure of freedom. In 1937 de Valera's Fianna Fáil government changed the state's title to Éire. It remained neutral during World War II and severed the last ties with Britain in 1949, becoming an independent republic. The policies of Taoiseach (prime minister) Seán Lemass (1899–1971) allowed Ireland to experience some of the general European economic boom of the 1960s. Now an active member of the European Union it has all the features, positive and negative, of a prosperous and increasingly urban and secular modern state, while still retaining a deserved reputation for achievement in music, drama and literature.

The state of Northern Ireland was tailored to the specifications of the unionists, the territory carefully chosen to make it economically viable but permanently under Protestant control. The six counties of Derry, Antrim, Down, Armagh, Tyrone and Fermanagh were partitioned off from the rest of the country with a border which became permanent in 1925 when the Boundary Commission's proposal to maintain the border was accepted by William Cosgrave (1880–1965), the political leader of the Free State's ruling party, Cumann na nGaedheal. The Northern Ireland government's main purpose (meeting in palatial buildings in Stormont in east Belfast) was to maintain the Union and keep those nationalists unfortunate enough to live in the six sequestered counties as an underclass. They succeeded because of the elaborate inattention of successive Westminster governments, but in the postwar welfare state with social security and educational opportunities in theory available to all, a politically-aware generation of Catholics grew up which was not prepared to accept their status as 'second-class citizens'.

In 1967 the Northern Ireland Civil Rights Association (NICRA) organised a series of protest marches, one of which was scheduled for Derry on 5 October 1968. It was banned by the

The Ardagh Chalice, a fine expression of 8th–century Irish metalwork
(National Museum of Ireland)

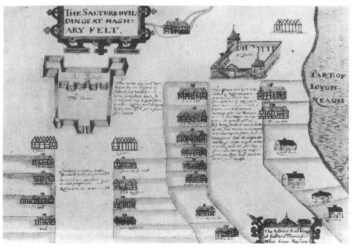

Map from Sir Thomas Phillips's survey of plantation villages
built in 1622 by the Salters' Company of London at Magherafelt
and Salterstown, County Derry

Michael Collins in 1917, soon after his release from the Frongoch prison camp in Wales, where he was detained for his activities during the Easter Rising of 1916 (Courtesy of Meda Ryan)

'O'Connell and his Contemporaries; the Clare election, 1828'
Painting by Joseph Haverty
(Reproduction courtesy of the National Gallery of Ireland)

Eviction scene in County Fermanagh, probably in the late 1880s
(Lawrence Collection, courtesy of the National Library of Ireland)

Irish Free State troops entering Portobello Barracks, Dublin,
18th May, 1922 (National Museum of Ireland)

The Battle of Antrim, the crucial battle in Ulster during 1798, in
which the United Irishmen were defeated

Ministry of Home Affairs and the marchers, refusing to accept the ban, were severely beaten by the RUC and the B-specials (an armed Protestant auxiliary force). The world news cameras recorded the unionist response to a peaceful march and that night there was serious rioting in Derry for the first time since 1920. Rioting and worse violence was to be repeated many times through the province and in time the Stormont monolith fell. By then the IRA, the political descendants of the irreconcilable rump of the Civil War Republicans, had resumed its 'armed struggle'. Internment followed in 1971. In Derry, thirteen men on an anti-internment march were shot dead by British paratroopers on 30 January 1972. This violence – and the subsequent evasions and cover-ups – caused many young Catholics to join the IRA and led to attacks upon the army, the police and the Ulster Defence Regiment. Since most of the personnel were Protestant, these attacks were seen as sectarian and led in turn to the resurrection of Protestant paramilitaries and increased sectarian strife. The bitter attrition lasted until 1994. Ceasefires were declared by the IRA and the Protestant UDA and UVF only to be broken again in February 1996 when two Londoners were killed in an explosion at Canary Wharf.

By then the government of the Republic had (despite the bitter resistance of many unionist politicians) assumed equal responsibility with the British parliament for affairs in the North, and Dáil politicians were assiduous in the efforts for what came to be called the 'peace process'. Bill Clinton, the colourful Democratic President of the US, associated his name with it and after intensive diplomacy a majority of unionists and nationalists accepted the Good Friday agreement (10 April 1998), which is a blueprint for detente and reconciliation in Northern Ireland affairs and a possible future without strife. The province is in a situation not unlike that of the Free State in 1923; there is a deep desire on the part of ordinary people for an end to death and injury, and some system of coexistence between Catholic and Protestant. Extremist rumps on both sides, for whom the heady wine of violence and armed power have become a staple, resent any compromise, and the killing of thirty people and the serious wounding of hundreds more in Omagh on 15 August 1998 by a splinter group calling themselves the Real IRA shows how much damage may be done by a few dissidents. The support by many Protestants of the Orange Order and their yearly sectarian rituals is also a cause for worry. Yet, unlike the situation in the 1920s, the ideal of peace has become a European, not to say an international responsibility. The Labour government of Tony Blair has a greater affinity with both the Dublin government and the nationalist Social Democratic and Labour Party (SDLP) than that which existed under the long rule of the Tories. And the joint acceptance of the Nobel Peace Prize by John Hume (b. 1937), the leader of the SDLP and unionist leader David Trimble (b. 1944) in October 1998 has both a symbolic and a real significance.

2

GAEL, GALL AND GALL-GAELACH

The early immigrations to Ireland, whether nomadic, mercantile or colonial, had ceased by the beginning of the Christian era. Though the country was small it was essentially trackless and where not boggy or rocky, heavily wooded, and there is no reason to suppose that the succeeding waves of 'takings' were bloody or resisted. Aboriginal groups, depending on their way of life, may very well have been allowed to continue relatively free of interference. The impressive megalithic remains, dolmens, passage graves and tumuli (especially those which were such a feature of the fertile Boyne valley) were left undisturbed by the people who came to dominate the island. The Gaels were *in situ* by 300 BC and well established as a nation by the time Christianity was brought from Britain and Gaul. They were the most cohesive group of the

Celtic people who, originating in south central Europe around 1000 BC, had spread east and west and were now peripherally sited in Scotland, Wales, the Isle of Man, Cornwall and Brittany as well as Ireland.

The Gaels were a warlike race of mainly stock breeders with a fine aesthetic sense and a delight in telling stories of 'those who lived here before'. The crumbling *imperium Romanum* had left Britain, Pictland and northwest Gaul unprotected and just as the Scandinavian freebooters were to do nearly a millennium later from the other direction these Gaels raided the west coasts of Britain, pillaged, took slaves and established trade routes. Christianity, the religion of the dying empire, probably first came to Ireland with British colonists. When St Patrick, who had himself been a slave, made Ireland his mission field in the fifth century, the Christianising was remarkably effective. The Gaelic temperament preferred a monastic system to the episcopal model which was the norm in other parts of Christendom and it was because of this idiosyncrasy that the Ireland of the second half of the first millennium gained its reputation as the 'Island of Saints and Scholars'.

Its monasteries were the island's first town-ships, containing within their protective palisades the usual amenities of urban life. They were also the country's universities, hospitals, workshops and sources of the recovery of the faith in pagan and heretical northern Europe. The paradox, as it seems to us today, is that all this spiritual, intellectual and aesthetic life coexisted with dynastic local struggles and a tendency towards civil war. The effect was that though no one could decry the courage or fierceness in battle of the Gaels, they had difficulty in conceiving any idea of national emergency, mainly because they were unaware of the idea of a nation. This was the pattern in the world as it was then known, but with the compact nature of the country and the sea as a clearly visible territorial boundary the Irish had less excuse than the Burgundians or the Piedmontese.

When the Scandinavians, driven by the need for *Lebensraum* at home, a tradition of 'raiding and trading' and a strong maritime instinct, began to turn their eyes westwards, the Christian islands were an obvious prey. The Norsemen were the fiercest fighters and finest mariners and inflicted most damage on Ireland, finding the monastic islands and peninsulas and the riverine settlements easy prey for their armoured longboats. The Danes, although just as swiftly ruthless, were more inclined to colonisation than sporadic raiding, and it was they who created Ireland's first seaports: Dublin, Wexford, Waterford and Limerick. Between 793, when the *Fionnghaill* (fair-haired foreigners) from Norway attacked Lindisfarne, and 1014 when the Leinstermen and the *Dúghaill* (dark-haired foreigners) were defeated by Brian Boru at the battle of Clontarf, they were a constant threat and cause of death, destruction and pillage. Yet they too, as had earlier waves of incomers, became assimilated, and continued as Christians to develop trade with Britain and Europe.

By 1154, when Henry II became king, England was by the standards of the time a united country and its king was also lord of large tracts of France. The power of the king was dependent on the loyalty of local barons and the most troublesome were those who held land along the Welsh border, the 'marcher' lords, many of whom were descended sinisterly from the fiercely prolific Welsh princess Nesta Ap Rhys. Henry had been granted overlordship of Ireland at his coronation by the English-born Pope Adrian IV, partly as a result of the well-intentioned denigration of the Irish by St Malachy to St Bernard of Clairvaux, and it was a project that he intended to develop.

The province of Leinster, still smarting from the old wounds inflicted by Brian Boru, was ruled in mid-twelfth century by Dermot Mac-Murrough (1110–c. 1171). His territorial ambitions, enmity with Rory O'Connor (d. 1198), the last *ard rí*, and his abduction (and return) of the willing Dervorgilla, wife of Ó Ruairc of Breifne, had caused him to be expelled from Ireland. His appeal to Henry gave the wily Plantagenet a chance to distract the unruly marcher lords, notably Richard 'Strongbow' de Clare, Robert Fitzstephen, Raymond Le Gros and Maurice Fitzgerald, and indicate to the world his right to the island. The Anglo-Normans' military successes in 1169 and 1170, the equivalent of tanks versus bows and arrows, made Henry realise that he must visit this latest possession and in 1171 he arrived at Waterford with 4,000 men to receive the submission not only of his barons but also of a significant numbers of Irish chieftains; after all, he was just another irrelevant *ard rí*. In 1175 Rory O'Connor came to Windsor to acknowledge Henry's sovereignty, and two years later Prince John was made Lord of Ireland.

The Anglo-Norman conquest changed the face of Gaelic Ireland: towns were built around sturdy stone castles, agriculture assumed an equal importance with stock-rearing and a reformed church, now episcopalian and ruled by four archdioceses, was at one not only with Rome but also with Canterbury. The 'conquest' was incomplete; by the end of the thirteenth century Ireland had three distinct elements of rule: the 'land of peace' which by Tudor times had shrunk to the counties controllable by Dublin, home of the loyal 'old English', the lands of the Anglo-Normans who eventually adopted Gaelic speech and lifestyle, and the essentially unconquered Gaelic kingdoms of the north and west. The independence of the realms outside of the steadily diminishing 'English land' increased, and later historians distinguished among the inhabitants of Ireland 'Gael', 'Gall-Gaelach' and 'Gall', the last being the generic term for foreigner. These realms enjoyed a relatively peaceful existence during this period with the exception of three turbulent events: Edward Bruce's efforts (1315–8) to become high-king, which ended with his death at the battle of Faughart; the Black Death (1348–9); and the several anti-English affrays of Art MacMurrough (1394, 1399).

By the time of the death of Richard III, 'the last English king', as Plantagenet supporters still revere him, at Market Bosworth in 1485, the leading Gall-Gaelach family were the Fitz-geralds, Earls of Kildare. Garret Mór had taken the Yorkist side in the Wars of the Roses and was arrested and imprisoned on suspicion of implication in Perkin Warbeck's attempt to dethrone Henry VII in 1497. The king's famous remark on making him Lord Deputy on his release in 1499 – 'Since all Ireland cannot rule this man, this man must rule all Ireland' – was an indication of his power and prestige. There was then a possible chance for independence with Fitzgerald as king but it would have been unlikely to have survived his death. Certainly Henry VIII's captains made short work of Garret Mór's son and grandson and Henry himself assumed the title of King of Ireland in 1541.

The Tudor conquest was about to begin, and it was the last unassimilable rump of all the 'takers', the Old English of the Pale, who had offered the crown to the now Protestant king. The process set in train by Henry was continued by his daughter Mary with her plantation of the O'More and O'Connor lands of Laois and Offaly, establishing in 1557 Queen's County and King's County in honour of her husband Philip II of Spain. It was pursued much more rigorously by his younger daughter Elizabeth I. Munster and Leinster were beaten into submission by her clinically ruthless armies but she was not to live to accept the submission of her erstwhile favourite Hugh O'Neill, quondam Earl of Tyrone and Baron Dungannon. The last invasion of Ireland had taken place; more than three hundred years were to pass before the heirs to the Tudor conquerors handed power back to the descendants of the native Gael and Gall-Gael whom they had supplanted.

3

FIGHTING BACK

By 1250, four-fifths of the country had been taken by the Gall. Only the rulers of the lands of O'Neill and O'Donnell kept the foreigners at bay, from 1257 supplementing their own forces with gallowglasses, famous Scot-Norse mercenaries from the Western Isles.

In 1315 in what was (like other rebellions to come) a combination of invasion and rebellion, a possible candidate for the high-kingship of Ireland arrived in the person of the Scottish Edward Bruce, the brother of Robert Bruce, the hero of Bannockburn. He landed at Larne and after successful campaigns in Antrim and Meath was crowned 'King of Ireland' on the hill of Knocknemelan near Dundalk in 1316. His soldiers were very effective (especially when he was joined briefly by his brother and his army) but, not having siege engines, he failed to take Dublin. He returned north and might have held Ulster and Meath for as long as it took for supplies and reinforcements to come from Scotland, but he unwisely engaged a much larger army under de Bermingham at Faughart in 1318. He was killed after a gallant fight and his men dispersed to find their own way home.

The kings of England from the time of Edward III (1337) to the middle of the reign of Henry VI (1453) had been fighting the Hundred Years' War with France and had little time for Irish affairs. This was followed, after an interval of only two years, by the thirty-year civil Wars of the Roses. During this time, the assimilation of the Anglo-Normans into the fabric of Irish life was consolidated and the Gall lost the precarious footholds they had established in the north and west of Ireland. When Henry VII became the first Tudor monarch after the Battle of Bosworth Field in 1485 and the English monarchy turned its attention westwards for the first time in decades, the effect was catastrophic both for the great Anglo-Norman families and for Gaelic Ireland. The Anglo-Normans, now styled Sean-Ghall or Old English, at first seemed impregnable. The Lord Deputy, Garret Mór Fitzgerald, the 'great Earl of Kildare' had supported the Yorkist side in the War of the Roses and continued to support in turn the pretenders Lambert Simnel and Perkin Warbeck after the accession of Henry VII. He was imprisoned in the Tower of London but released in 1499 after Warbeck's execution. Henry restored him as deputy, having decided that 'since all Ireland cannot rule this man, this man must rule all Ireland.' Garret Mór was succeeded by his son Gearóid Óg, but by then Henry VII was dead and his second son, Henry VIII, was on the throne of England. Kildare spent several periods in the Tower of London while his loyalty was dissected and he finally died there in 1534.

The first real act of military defiance of the Tudor era was undertaken by Lord Offaly, the son of Garret Óg, ninth Earl of Kildare. 'Silken Thomas' as he is better known, had more dash but much less diplomacy than his father or grandfather and was soon engaging a English army under Sir William Skeffington, who had been appointed deputy to succceed Garret Óg in 1534. Skeffington slaughtered all the surrendered garrison of the Kildare ancestral home at Maynooth including the clerical chaplains, establishing a reputation for extreme ruthlessness that was to characterise many Tudor captains in Ireland. There would be more 'Maynooth Pardons'. Thomas, briefly tenth Earl of Kildare, was executed with his five uncles at Tyburn, all six hanged, drawn and quartered as traitors and heretics on 3 February 1537.

With the Kildare Fitzgeralds no longer a threat and his third wife Jane Seymour having produced the desired male heir, Henry VIII felt himself able to ease the vigour of his Irish campaigns. He settled for persuasion, and received the submission of Old English and Gaelic lords who hailed him King of Ireland.

Like her father, Elizabeth I, who succeeded to the English throne in 1558, would have preferred to pacify Ireland by negotiation rather than conquest. The O'Neills in their Ulster fastnesses were the premier Gaelic family, and showed the classical pattern of internal dissension and fierce enmity with rivals. But the 'great'

O'Neill, Hugh, Earl of Tyrone, for many years seemed content to keep the Queen's peace. In the decade 1573–83 there were risings in Munster, Queen's and King's Counties (modern-day Laois and Offaly) and Wicklow, which achieved little. All, but especially the outbreaks in the south-west, were put down with exemplary savagery, by Lord Deputy Grey de Wilton and by Perrott, Ormond and Carew. There were few battles, the campaign rather consisting of sieges and massacres, including the killing in 1580 at Smerwick near Ballyferriter in the Dingle peninsula of a mixed force of seven hundred Spaniards and Italians sent by Pope Gregory XIII and Philip II of Spain. Following the desolation of the Desmond rebellion, 210,000 acres of good Munster land was confiscated – 'relinquished' by the attainted earl and his supporters. The pattern of rebellion followed by confiscation followed by plantation was to become familiar over the following century.

The great Tudor rebel Hugh O'Neill led a cavalry troop against the Desmonds in 1569 but had assumed the title 'The O'Neill' at the prehistoric inauguration stone at Tullyhogue near Cookstown in 1595, thereby effectively throwing the gauntlet down at Elizabeth's feet. He probably realised that the personal accommodation that he had made with Elizabeth might, like Gaelic chieftainship, end either at her death or at his. O'Neill was a fine captain who had learned the value of the new weapons of war, especially cannon and explosives, and he was able to rally great support from the other chieftains, even from his hereditary enemies, the O'Donnells, by suggesting that any war against England would be a religious one. Elizabeth reluctantly declared him a traitor and sent a number of commanders against him. He defeated Sir John Norris at Clontibret on 13 June 1595 and would have routed his army except that he ran out of shot. Three years later at the Yellow Ford, near Armagh, the combined armies of O'Neill, Red Hugh O'Donnell and Hugh Maguire of Fermanagh inflicted on Sir Henry Bagenal the severest defeat ever sustained by an English army in Ireland.

O'Neill dealt with the next Tudor champion even more conclusively; Robert Devereux, second Earl of Essex, was humiliated at Aclint on the

Louth-Monaghan border when his army of 20,000 troops was dismissed, at the start of a truce engineered by a supremely confident Tyrone. It was the start of a downward spiral which would lead to Essex's disgrace and death in 1601. But Essex's replacement as lord deputy was to be O'Neill's nemesis. Charles Blount, Lord Mountjoy, was a superior strategist and commanded a much better equipped army than O'Neill. His policy was a kind of summary of Tudor captains' tactics with destruction of property and burning of crops added to the usual slaughter of all opponents. His deliberate desecration of the Tullyhogue stone and the burning of Dungannon in 1602 were effective in driving O'Neill out of Ulster and making his struggle a countrywide crusade. Philip III of Spain promised help, but when del Águila's force arrived it landed at the entirely inappropriate port of Kinsale.

O'Neill, persuaded by the flamboyant O'Donnell, marched through an Ireland in the grip of a bitter winter and succeeded in getting between Mountjoy and his supply line to Cork. The most appropriate tactic was to starve the superior English army into submission but, as ever, the impatient Irish armies had neither stomach nor proper equipment for a siege. The attrition did not suit the Spaniards either, and against his will and better judgement O'Neill, whose successes had been achieved mainly by ambush and mobility, consented to a formal battle. The opposing forces met on the morning of Christmas Eve, 1601. It was all over in three hours and Gaelic Ireland had received its death blow. O'Neill retreated north and Red Hugh left for Spain. O'Neill finally surrendered to Mountjoy in March 1603, unaware that Elizabeth had died. Although the peace terms of the Treaty of Mellifont were more generous than he had a right to expect, his power and influence in his home province steadily diminished until he and other potentates of the province left Ireland for good in 1607 in what has become known as the 'Flight of the Earls'. Ugo, Conte di Tirone, was received kindly by Pope Paul V and lived until 1616 as a pensionary of the Spanish king.

The Ulster plantation that followed the Flight of the Earls succeeded better than any previous initiatives but it did not achieve its purpose of removing the disloyal natives. In fact the disloyalty – the perfidy – of their Catholic neighbours, tenants and servants is an unsheakable part of the mythology of the Protestant people of the province. In 1641, with England on the brink of civil war and the crown – and head – of Charles I in grave danger, the Catholic landowners in Ireland, both Old English and Old Irish, sensing that dissensions in Britain might give them an opportunity, decided to emulate the Scots and show some armed force. Plans to seize Dublin Castle were discovered on 22 October, the eve of the appointed day, but the risings in Ulster under Sir Phelim O'Neill and in Leinster led by Sir Rory O'More were initially successful. The dispossessed Irish turned on their masters. 2,000 Protestant settlers were killed, while many thousands more were stripped, dispossessed and 'driven into the waste'. The massacre marked the beginnings of a struggle of extreme complexity that involved, in varying permutations, the dispossessed Irish, the many Old Irish who still retained their lands, the Old English, the New English, the Ulster Scots, English and Scots armies of king and parliament, the churches and Archbishop Rinuccini, the representative of the Counter Reformation. The conflict would not end until the country was settled by the New Model Army. Its leaders, Oliver Cromwell, his son Henry, his son-in-law, Henry Ireton, and Edmund Ludlow, imposed a near-final solution as there had been no real opposition since the early death of the only efficient military leader, Owen Roe O'Neill (?1590–1649). His was the major military success of the eleven-year struggle, when he defeated the Scots under Robert Monro at Benburb, but his successor, Bishop Heber MacMahon, was no general. He was captured after a defeat near Letterkenny and executed in Enniskillen on 17 September 1650.

In Ireland Cromwell is the great Satan who slaughtered Drogheda, Wexford and Clonmel and completed the Tudor transfer of land from Irish to British proprietors. The Irish who were innocent of involvement in the war still had their lands confiscated, but they were conceded small estates west of the Shannon, such as should have neither coastal nor riparian access. 34,000 soldiers were allowed to leave the country with their officers and there was some selling of native Irish into West Indian slavery. The poor were, in general, allowed to continue undisturbed being poor.

The seventeeth century, a period in which some of the greatest upheavals of English history were fought out partly on Irish soil, ended with an Irish rebellion subsumed into what was to become known as 'the war of the three kings'. When James II was deposed in favour of his daughter Mary and her Protestant husband William of Orange, he fled to France, then landed as King of Ireland in Kinsale in March 1689 with a small French army which joined forces with a Catholic Irish army provided by his deputy Richard Talbot, Earl of Tyrconnell. It was to be the last decisive stand by Protestant Europe against the Counter Reformation and it was, unfortunately for Irish Catholics, successful. At Derry, Aughrim, Enniskillen and the Boyne, to use the Orange chant which makes up in euphony what it lacks in chronological sequence, 'our freedom, religion and laws' were safeguarded forever. It was as 'near-run' a thing as Waterloo, especially at Aughrim, but Ginkel's defeat of the French-Irish army settled the matter and Irish Ireland entered a cryonic state from which the waking was to be unconscionably slow and painful. After 'Aughrim's great disaster' more than a hundred years of apparent suspended animation had to be suffered before a new Ireland should, in the words of one of her best midwives, be 'a nation once again'.

After a century of Penal laws and economic if not religious oppression of the majority Catholics, a significant point in the development of a sense of nationhood was reached at the end of the eighteenth century and manifested in the various uprisings that collectively are known as the 1798 Rebellion. The association known as the United Irishmen had been founded in Belfast on 14 October 1791 by a group of young radicals, Wolfe Tone, Henry Joy McCracken, Samuel Neilson, William Drennan and others who were fired with ideas of reform. They were lawyers, merchants, journalists and were as blissful as Wordsworth at the fall of the Bastille. The country seemed to be aflame with radical ideas and grim with the need to keep them in check. The various branches of the United Irishmen (a Dublin society had been formed a month after the Belfast one, led by Napper Tandy and Hamilton Rowan) continued to debate the condition of the country and to call for reform.

The Dublin branch of the United Irishmen

was suppressed on 23 May 1794 and as an underground and secret society it attracted a larger and more ruthless membership with the kind of *sans-culottes* element that had been the terror of the Terror. In exile in France Wolfe Tone managed to persuade Carnot, the leading member of the revolutionary governing committee, to give him a general, Lazare Hoche, and an army of 15,000 men. They sailed for Bantry Bay in forty-three ships in December 1796. The expedition failed because of winter storms and the ships were forced to return home. The Bantry venture was and remains another of the great 'if onlys' or 'what ifs' of Irish history. The United Irishmen still flourished in Ulster, and March 1797 saw the start of a campaign by General Lake to root out radicalism. His powers were absolute and his methods of an extreme ruthlessness, including fire, torture and hanging carried out by an enthusiastic yeomanry.

Government swoops in Leinster in May 1798 badly weakened the society there and the week of 23–30 May saw unsuccessful actions in Naas, Clane, Lucan, Tallaght, Lusk, Rathfarnham, Monasterevin, Kilkenny, Slane, Baltinglass and Tara. The informers had done their business

well. The story in Wexford was different. There
was there a great deal of Protestant–Catholic
bitterness and a sufficient body of Catholic
farmers and artisans, not badly armed and with
a competent leader in Bagenal Harvey (1762–
98). At first the insurgents, with help from
contingents from Waterford and Carlow, met
with some success, and Harvey was able to
control his ragged followers with threats of
death for all guilty of 'excesses'. He was relieved
of his post after failing to capture New Ross on
5 June. The last engagement was at Vinegar Hill
in Enniscorthy, when Lake's forces overwhelmed
the 'rebels' on 21 June.

Hearing of the risings in the southeast, on
7 June McCracken led a party to attack Antrim,
but after some initial success was defeated by
Colonel Durham's militia. The other show of
defiance was at Ballynahinch, when Henry
Monro held out against General Nugent's army
for three days (11–13 June) before being hanged
in front of his own house in Lisburn on 15 June.
By the end of the month the "98 rising', as it
was later called, was virtually over. Harvey had
been hanged on Wexford Bridge on 26 June and
resprisals were in progress. The total death toll,

often because of naked sectarianism, was finally computed at around 30,000.

There were a few dramatic sideshows, one tragic, another farcical. Tone, assiduous as ever in France, managed to gather French forces for a landing at Killala under General Humbert on 22 August. The French set up the Republic of Connacht and defeated the government forces at the famous 'Races of Castlebar' five days later. On 8 September, after a fortnight of ragged skirmishing, Humbert surrendered to Lake and Cornwallis at Ballinamuck, County Longford, and his Irish followers, mostly Mayo peasants who had never been United Irishmen, were slaughtered. A small force accompanied by the egregious Napper Tandy landed at Rutland Island opposite Burton-port in west Donegal on 16 September, but hearing of Humbert's surrender Tandy got blind drunk and was carried back to his ship. He eventually escaped with his life, largely through the insistence of Napoleon. Finally Tone, found in the company of yet another French force, under Bompard, was arrested by the British navy on 20 September, tried and condemned to death. He slit his own throat and died a week later on 19 November.

The summer and autumn of 1798 had seen the greatest shedding of blood in Ireland's history, much of it in Wexford and nearly all of it sectarian. The rising there was more in the nature of a peasant's revolt over bread-and-butter issues, such as taxes, land and religious hatred. The events of the year 1798 were to form a significant part of the mythology that replaced historiography in the nationalist imagination from the 1840s on. The bravery of the insurgents was undeniable and the memory of sectarian excesses was muted by the bloody savagery of the reprisals. After a century of quiescence at injustice, a psychological dam had burst. Grattan's poignant address to the Ireland of the shotgun marriage of the Union, 'I see her in a swoon, but she is not dead', was truer than he realised. The dispossessed were at last on the move; Yeats's intermittently rough beast had begun its slouch towards Bethlehem.

Pitt could now say that his worst nightmare had materialised. Ireland was a 'ship on fire' but his remedy was extinguishment rather than cutting adrift. The Act of Union with Great Britain which denied the Irish the remedy of even a corrupt and bigoted parliament of their

own, was one of the most immediate con-
sequences of the bloody events of 1798. But the
rebellion was not entirely over. Robert Emmet
(1778–1803), who with Wolfe Tone became one
of the great heroes of the physical force school
of republicanism, was the younger brother of
Thomas Addis Emmet, the leading counsel for
the United Irishmen. In the mood that Yeats
later characterised as the 'delirium of the brave'
he led a crowd of Dublin 'Liberty Rangers' to
attack Dublin Castle on 23 July 1803. Lord
Kilwarden, the liberal chief justice, and his son-
in-law were dragged from their coach and
murdered. There was a skirmish in the Coombe
but the event quickly petered out and Emmet
fled to hiding in the mountains. Arrested on 25
August by Major Sirr, at the house in the village
of Harold's Cross where he had a tryst with
Sarah Curran, he was defended eloquently by
Leonard McNally, the author of 'Sweet Lass of
Richmond Hill' and the government's chief spy
during the whole of the United Irishmen episode.
He was hanged in Thomas Street on 20 September and decapitated the following day. His
'epitaph' speech from the dock and the romantic
trappings of his adventure made him the 'darling

of Erin' for nearly two hundred years. His friend Tommy Moore immortalised the lovers in two of his Irish Melodies, 'She Is Far from the Land' and 'O, Breathe Not His Name!', with which he later delighted liberal audiences in London.

Daniel O'Connell, who was Ireland's first great constitutional leader, gave the people their first real sense of nationhood when through mass meetings Catholics achieved some limited franchise for themselves. One of the great conundrums of Irish history is whether, had the Great Famine not occurred, the road to self-determination might have been a peaceful rather than an intermittently violent one. But the perceived 'attempted genocide' of the black 1840s had to be avenged, or so it seemed to the more stridently self-conscious heirs of Young Ireland, the dreamers of the 1840s. Many of those involved in the failed – even farcical – Young Ireland rising of 1848 escaped to France or America and continued with revolutionary zeal undiminished to plan for the physical force option which they believed was the only means of making Britain concede independence. In 1858, ten years after the Young Ireland débâcle at Ballingarry, John O'Mahony (1816–77) suggested

to James Stephens (1825–1901) the foundation
of a new republican organisation, at first known
as the the Irish Revolutionary Brotherhood and
later as the Irish Republican Brotherhood. Stephens
was to organise at home, while O'Mahony would
be in charge of the American arm. Because of
their stoicism in imprisonment, their domin-
ance of the English media during the 1860s and
their requisition by Pearse as revolutionary icons,
the names of O'Donovan Rossa, John Devoy,
T. C. Luby, Charles Kickham, Michael Doheny,
John O'Leary and Michael Davitt are still entities
in an emotional hall of fame. They were soon
called 'Fenians' after the Fianna of Fionn Mac
Cumhaill in the saga, the name originating in
New York.

Stephens, who loved the idea of a secret
society with its cells and oaths, was a notable
procrastinator, and the 1865 insurrection – which
was to be the more effective because of arms and
trained men from America and timed to take
place on 20 September, the anniversary of
Emmet's rising – had to be aborted. On 15
September O'Leary, Luby and Rossa were
arrested. The turn of Stephens and Kickham
came on 11 November, and John Devoy, who

took over command from Stephens, was imprisoned the following February. Prison conditions were made deliberately harsh and Kickham's health was broken after he had served four of his fourteen years' penal servitude. O'Donovan Rossa, Devoy, O'Leary, Luby all served at least five years before being released on condition of exile. Stephens had escaped from Richmond Gaol a fortnight after his arrest.

The IRB had gained grudging respect, and its activities, apart from a few uncoordinated and short-lived affrays in Kerry, Louth, Wicklow, Tipperary, Cork, Limerick and Clare in March 1867, consisted mainly of attempted rescues of members. On 11 September Thomas Kelly and Timothy Deasy, now heads of the movement, were arrested in Manchester and one week later in a successful rescue attempt from a prison van in Manchester a police sergeant called Charles Brett was accidentally shot. Three Fenians, Philip Allen, Michael Larkin and Michael O'Brien were tried for his murder and hanged on 23 November. It was an age of instant ballads and 'God Save Ireland', which told of the 'gallant three' forever known as the 'Manchester Martyrs', attained almost the status of a national anthem.

The 'bold Fenian men' had for the time being been defeated. Factionalism followed and there were to be several localised eruptions organised by ever-smaller splinter groups. A group significantly calling itself the 'Irish Republican Army' had invaded Canada at the end of May 1866. It was led by John O'Neill, a former Union general and Indian fighter who soon after his brief imprisonment abandoned further republican activity. One of the Fenian oaths started with the words: 'I do solemnly swear allegiance to the Irish Republic, *now virtually established* . . . '[emphasis mine]. This arrogation of sovereignty was to establish the moral right to carry on a war as if a country called the Republic of Ireland actually existed. It was a right later assumed by the IRA and so stated in 1920, 1938 and 1971. The undefined Fenian tradition lived on, regularly to reawaken the Phoenix Flame, as O'Donovan Rossa called the cause. It was at his graveside in August 1915 that the retiring, far from oratorical Padraig Pearse delivered a speech that is widely credited with fanning the Fenian flame into armed rebellion for the new century: 'The fools, the fools, they have left us our Fenian dead.' So was revived a use of physical force in the name of freedom that long outlived what many would see as even the doubtful legitimacy of the Easter Rising and the War of Independence.

The IRB had been rekindled by the old Fenian Thomas J. Clarke (1857–1916) who had, at the age of fifty, been sent to Dublin by John Devoy (1842–1928), the king over the water, head of Clan na Gael in New York. His tobacconist shop in what is now Parnell Street became the nerve centre of his operations and by 1915 an armed rising was in plan. As ever, 'England's difficulty' was to be 'Ireland's opportunity.' The supreme council included Clarke, Sean MacDermott (1884–1916), Eamonn Ceannt (1881–1916) and Pearse (1879–1916). The latter three were prominent members of the now highly politicised Gaelic League. The late colonial administrator Roger Casement (1864–1916), also sponsored by John Devoy, went to Berlin to look for possible members of an Irish Brigade to be formed from prisoners of war, but without success. The IRB was in fact a tiny organisation, although there were cells in most parts of the country.

The date was fixed for Easter Monday, 24

April 1916, against the advice of most members of the Irish Volunteers and of Casement, who felt that no move should be made without a substantial number of German troops. The arms that were to come in the German ship, the *Aud*, were lost when the captain scuttled her on arrest by a British naval patrol in Tralee Bay on 21 April, and Casement, landing at Banna Strand, near Fenit in County Kerry, with instructions to cancel the rising, was arrested. MacNeill, after many misgivings, first approved then vetoed the venture, and cancelled all the planned syn-chronous sympathetic local outbreaks. In the end about 1,600 men, including 300 members of the Irish Citizen Army, occupied various buildings in Dublin, including famously the General Post Office. Pearse read a proclamation entitled *The Proclamation of the Government of the Irish Republic to the People of Ireland* from the steps of the GPO. They held out until the Saturday when Pearse surrendered to General Lowe.

The authorities' reaction of execution of the leaders was unwise but perhaps inevitable given the emotional heightening caused by the war in Europe. Even more ominous was the imposition of martial law by General Maxwell. More people were arrested than had taken part in the rising. When the rebels had been marched away they had to run a gauntlet of jeering Dubliners who had spent Easter week looting from the damaged stores. Yet by the first weeks of May, when fifteen of the leaders had been shot in what seemed like a sequence deliberately paced for maximum effect, and Casement, awaiting trial in Pentonville, was having the details of his homosexual diaries revealed by the attorney-general, F. E. Smith, the mood of city and country had in Yeats's phrase 'changed utterly'; a terrible beauty – or something – had been born.

Eventually wiser counsels prevailed. None of the remaining seventy-four insurgents who had been condemned to death at the courts martial was executed and most of the 1,800 who were interned were released by the end of 1917.

In Dublin the results of the 1918 general election led to the setting up of the independent parliament, Dáil Éireann, on 21 January 1919. On the same day a guerrilla war masterminded by Michael Collins (1890–1922) but conducted by quasi-independent local units began. The pistol that had been cocked in 1916 was now about to have its trigger pulled.

By September 1919 a state of insurrection existed, the IRA using localised 'flying columns' as their main means of attack. The government, now led by Lloyd George, responded with flinty heavy-handedness. The behaviour of the two specially assembled British forces, the Black-and-Tans and the Auxies, was such that world opinion turned quickly against Britain. As the war continued, the ferocity of the reprisals increased with each IRA attack.

Eventually after months of killings, reprisals, burnings and a countrywide climate of fear, Lloyd George gave in to international pressure and general moral affront at home and a truce came into effect on 11 July 1921. The Treaty that was signed on 6 December 1921 brought into being the partitioned Irish Free State (Saorstát Éireann) and for most Irish people ended forever the legitimacy of the physical force philosophy in the struggle for independence.

4

THE BLACK NORTH

Recently there appeared a piece of gable art in loyalist East Belfast. It showed Cúchulainn, the hero of Ulster, as the defender of the North against the rest of Ireland. It was a nice piece of political opportunism and there was a kind of (superficial) mythic truth about it. The folk memory that is the source of all the Irish sagas recalls an Ireland where internecine conflict was common; but to use inappropriate modern terms it was as likely to be intercounty as inter-provincial, and certainly not the North against the rest.

The otherness of Ulster that figures in more subtle unionist propaganda which takes it to be a region separate from the rest of Ireland has some historical and topographical basis. The swathe of drumlins, a legacy from the Ice Age, which stretches from Carlingford and Strangford Loughs to Donegal Bay, acted as a natural barrier, strengthened by the prehistoric earthworks known as the Black Pig's Dyke and the woods, bogs and lakes of the north midlands. The closeness of Scotland meant that the inhabitants were as likely to look north and east as south, and journeys to Galloway or Kintyre were probably easier than to Leinster. These natural barriers did give the northern lands a sense, if not of isolation, then of autonomy.

The popularity of the cult of the queen-deity Macha (who named Armagh) made the settlement that bears her name a suitable centre of rule for the Patrician church but it would be many years before the reforms of Malachy rendered it an effective and acceptable primatial see. The Scandinavian raiders used Strangford and Carlingford (the names they brought with them) and made their way up Lough Foyle to attack the monastery established by Saint Columb, but they were not inclined to found towns there as they did in the south and east. The later Norman invaders did what they could to subdue the Gael by building castles at Carlingford,

Carrickfergus and Northburgh (Greencastle near Moville in Inishowen), but fifty years after John de Courcy (d. *c.* 1219) had declared himself *Princeps Ulidiae* (Prince of Ulster) the Gall had lost most of their conquered lands. They held peripheral coastal enclaves at Coleraine, Carrickfergus and Downpatrick but ceased to have a significant say in the northern province. The Gael was once again supreme.

The ancient Gaelic lifestyle persisted in Ulster right up to the time of the sixteenth-century Tudor conquest (the people of the west coast of Scotland had the same pattern of government, the same language and the same tendency to wage war on each other). The O'Neill sovereignty based in what is now County Tyrone had survived the destruction of the houses of Kildare and Desmond and it was Elizabeth I's fond hope that Hugh O'Neill, who had received an English education and been made Earl of Tyrone and Baron Dungannon, might rule the province for her in peace. In spite of his long war which ended in the defeat at Kinsale (1601), his surrender at Mellifont in 1603 allowed him to retain his position. By then the Stuart James I had begun to examine a plan for plantation drawn up by Sir John Davies (1569–1626), and when O'Neill left the province for permanent exile in Rome in 1607 the way was open for a means of pacification which, though less dramatic than military conquest, would destroy the Gaelic structure by the confiscation of the lands of the disloyal.

Lord Deputy Chichester had already begun an unofficial seeding of south Antrim and north Down with undertakers and was anxious for a system of regrant which would keep the native people of Ulster on roughly their own lands. He was overruled, and the counties of Donegal, Londonderry (originally Coleraine), Armagh, Cavan, Tyrone and Fermanagh were parcelled out to volunteer undertakers, a city to be called Londonderry to be the responsibility of the London companies. The planters were English and Scots, the latter mainly Presbyterian farmers from Galloway and Argyle who regarded themselves as emigrants to a wilderness that they would tame, risking the incursions of the dispossessed. They survived the Rising of 1641 and lived in relative peace until the Williamite

Wars, when the unsuccessful Siege of Derry (1688–9) proved an ominous prophecy of the defeat of James II's forces at the Boyne and Aughrim.

After the Treaty of Limerick, the Catholic population was all but crushed by the system of Penal Laws which were passed between 1695 and 1728, but they were still required as labourers on the neat farms and in the tidy towns that made eighteenth-century Ulster look so different from other parts of Ireland. (Many more Scots immigrants came to Ulster in the decade after Limerick than in the previous century.) The curse of absentee landlordism had considerably less effect because of a more enlightened system of tenure (called the 'Ulster custom'), and the encouragement of the linen trade, mechanised by such refugee Huguenots as Samuel-Louis Crommelin (1652–1727), essentially changed the character of the northern province. The established Church of Ireland, which was numerically superior, was entitled to tithes from all landholders and the Presbyterians, though not penalised to the same extent as Catholics, were still regarded as dissenters.

The legendary industry of Protestant Ulster people (and of a growing urban population of successful Catholic businessmen) encouraged trade, and the resulting prosperity and concomitant leisure meant that Enlightenment ideas were by the end of the eighteenth century a significant feature of life in Belfast, Derry and other urban centres. The effect of the successful revolution in America (to which emigrant Ulstermen, mainly Presbyterians seeking full religious and political freedom, had vigorously contributed) and the apparent end of the *ancien régime* in France encouraged radical ideas in Belfast. It was there that the Society of United Irishmen was founded in 1791 by Wolfe Tone (1763–98), Thomas Russell (1767–1803) and Samuel Neilsen (1761–1803), and vigorously opposed by the county yeomanries, usually members of the anti-Catholic Orange Order, which had been founded in 1795.

Risings in Antrim and Down led by Henry Joy McCracken (1767–98) and Henry Monro (1758–98), were quite soon put down and the leaders executed, and a still prosperous Ulster accepted the Act of Union with general jubilation.

The revolutionary fervour of Presbyterians became muted in the long peace and continuing prosperity of the favoured province. The fervour of preacher Henry Cooke (1788–1868) routed the Arian heresy which had characterised the more liberal wing of the faith and reconciled the majority to unionism. With all penalties removed and the Church of Ireland disestablished in 1869, Presbyterians so far forgot their radical tradition as to join the Orange Order. Belfast, the loyal city, and the 'sound' Lagan Valley were advanced industrially not only at the expense of the nationalist western counties of Fermanagh and Tyrone but even at the expense of Dublin. Though lacking any natural hinterland of coal or iron deposits, Belfast became as industrialised as Birmingham or Glasgow, and gained a worldwide reputation for shipbuilding.

The North was therefore the part of Ireland where unionism not only worked but seemed a *source* of material prosperity. Relatively unaffected by the Famine in the Protestant east and already having the system of tenure for which the Land War was fought, there were, as it seemed to the unionist majority, no advantages to be gained by the various Home Rule bills brought forward by Liberal premiers and distinct disadvantages, including the voiced objection to 'Rome Rule' and the real terror of economic slump. The founding of the UVF in 1913 and the rise of Sinn Féin after the 1916 Rising made partition, offered by Lloyd George (1863–1945) to prevent a north-south civil war, acceptable. The favourable terms of the choice of the six counties of Ulster that would be economically viable while maintaining unionist supremacy were eventually won by the adamant attrition of James Craig. The anomalous state of Northern Ireland came into being in 1920. Nationalist objections were quelled in a short sharp civil war when the UVF, now known as the 'B'-special constabulary, and the British Army effectively silenced any slight IRA resistance.

The monolithic state of Northern Ireland was grounded in overt equality for all citizens. But subtle electoral boundary-drawing, economic zoning and a 'green' ceiling for Catholic preferment meant that the minority population were kept effectively an underclass. The violent birth of the state and the siege mentality that still characterises most unionists produced the Special Powers Act in 1922 and its being made permanent in 1933 gave the authorities such capacity as to make it the envy of other repressive governments (notably that of South Africa). The welfare provisions of the postwar Labour government applied also in Northern Ireland so that Catholics benefited from free secondary and third-level education. Catholics, prevented from normal advancement in industry, business and the local civil and municipal service, had already used education as a way round the 'invisible' sectarian discrimination. The other welfare provisions in health, family allowances, unemployment and national assistance in fact aided Catholics more than the rest since they were more likely to have large families and be out of work. One effect was that the rate of emigration of Catholics that had characterised the statelet since its foundation sharply decreased.

In Northern Ireland the economic miracle of the 1960s was largely kept for the 'loyal' areas east of the Bann river, which since prehistoric times had acted as a natural division of the province. The mood of the period and the new-found prosperity led a generation of politically aware and educated Catholics to action with demands for civil rights and an end to the malpractice of the Stormont government. The violence of government response and the presence of the world's cameras shattered the monolithic structure of unionism. Although Operation Harvest (1956–62), the most recent border campaign of the IRA, had been speedily defeated, there were enough old campaigners still around to begin again, especially with a large number of eager youths from working-class areas in cities and rural republican enclaves anxious to renew the 'armed struggle'. The attacks on Catholic areas in Belfast in the summer of 1969 and the continuous rioting in Derry after the Apprentice Boys' march in August led to the introduction of the British Army on the streets to keep the peace, soon becoming an obvious target as an 'occupying force'.

The renewed IRA campaign led to internment without trial on 9 August 1971 and the killing of anti-internment marchers in Derry on Bloody Sunday (30 January 1972) resulted in huge republican recruitment. The next twenty-five years were marked by bombings, attacks on the security forces, especially the RUC and Ulster Defence Regiment, most of whose personnel were Protestant, and any people deemed by the paramilitaries to be ancillary workers. Protestants rejected the IRA's sophistry that they were a non-sectarian force (there were Catholics among their targets too) and continued to attack Catholics, rather more indiscriminately. The present uneasy peace based on an agreement brokered by the London and Dublin governments with input from the EU and the US is still at risk from old unionist intransigence on the one side, constitutionally centred in Ian Paisley's Democratic Unionist Party (DUP) and in the naked sectarianism of some elements of the Orange Order, and on the other, in the diehard tradition of the eternal 'armed struggle' notably in the 'Continuity' IRA.

The original demands of the Northern Ireland Civil Rights Association of 1968 have all been granted and the prospect of the answer to the wearisome Irish Question being found is greater now than at any time in the island's history. The Dublin government is no longer in a position to make pious anti-partitionist remarks its only contribution to a solution of the problem, as it could in the early decades of its freedom, and most nationalists have learned to respect the traditions and empathise with the fears of the Protestant majority. These feel betrayed and they have found it harder as people who have been in a privileged position for four hundred years to learn to think the unthinkable. The peace process has its own momentum and, with Tony Blair as prime minister and Mo Mowlam as a charismatic (and lucky) minister, there is reason for cautious optimism. The most potent factor working for peace is war fatigue and the longing for the good old days when Northern Ireland was to the casual eye an elegant and worthy part of the United Kingdom.

5

DECLINE AND REVIVAL
IN LANGUAGE AND CULTURE

Many people have sought to understand how a tiny island off the west coast of Europe with a damp climate and a history both eventful and tragic could have contributed to the world – and should continue to contribute – such literary and intellectual riches. Irish literature in English, much of which dates from the past two centuries, is one of the jewels in the crown of western civilisation, while most contemporary readers, even Irish readers, will be unable to access in the original tongue any of the riches of Gaelic literature and poetry. For Ireland to have produced in this century alone Yeats, Joyce, Beckett and Heaney (three of these being Nobel laureates) is astonishing; add to this list Wilde, Synge, Kavanagh and a multitude of practitioners in all the literary genres and bafflement grows rather than diminishes. Ireland is famous too for music, music that is traditional – in the sense of owing little to formal education or written notation but that is handed on orally – whether performed on a fiddle, accordion or by the voice. This is a gift virtually unique in the developed world, a gift possessed by many Irish musicians. And recently the Irish have proven themselves adept at making business of culture, whether through the performance of *Riverdance* or simply the marketing of Dublin as a fashionable tourist destination.

The Donegal-born poet William Allingham (1824–89), although he found the 'Kelts' very congenial, could not bring himself to write a history of Ireland: 'lawlessness and turbulency, robbery and oppression, hatred and revenge, blind selfishness everywhere – no principle, no heroism. What can be done with it?' Few would dispute that the scars of events like the Great Famine of 1845–7 are real or that the Civil War of 1922–3 still has the power to hurt and sadden. The most distressful country is successful, creative, abundant, perhaps despite

herself, despite the loss of her people (a haemor-
rhage staunched only in recent decades) and the
loss of her own language. In any search for the
roots of Irish culture it is to the Celts that we
must look – those nomadic and warlike invaders
who came to Ireland from south-central Europe.

The Celts' fascination with those they perceived as their own particular ancestors seems
positively Shintoist. They held in their imagin-
ations a heroic age with epic warriors and
conflicts, and queens as powerful and independent as any king. By the fifth century they had
a common language; a version of *ur*-Celtic that
finally became Irish, Manx and Gaelic. In this
language they created, memorised and passed
down by word of mouth marvellous tales about
what they held as their past. The great prose and
verse epic *Táin Bó Cuailgne* which tells of a
struggle between Connacht's Queen Medb and
Ulster's King Conchubar and describes the death
of Cú Chulainn, the greatest of the northern
heroes, may have its origin in the struggle which
pushed the historical Ulaid east of the Bann.

The pre-Christian society was a hierarchical
one with clear class distinctions, a fine sense of

aesthetic design and an unusual respect for poetry, traditional lore (including genealogy) and storytelling. The poets shared with scholars, physicians, jurists, top artificers and scholars membership of the *aes dána* (men of art) whose social stratum was fixed between that of nobles and free commoners.

The society which the Christian missionaries found was not unaware of religion. It had its gods and goddesses who lived in the Otherworld, a kind of idealised life on earth where all appetites were satisfied. The people believed that death was the end only of the body and that a life of the spirit continued in another place. Their worship of the sun and the spirits of rivers and lakes indicated a pleasure in the natural world and this characterised their vernacular poetry when they found the means to write it down. They made their ancestors into heroes and their heroes into gods. When Patrick and the other missionaries brought Christianity, the Irish recognised a belief not at all alien. They took to it in time and subtly altered its practice to suit their temperaments. Their attitude to life, in so far as we can judge it, was on the whole honourable, cheerful and sensual. Divorce was prevalent and the practice of polygamy among the noble class persisted until Tudor times. In general their theology was wary but not fearful. The Gaelic way of life, modified and sensitised by the adopted faith, survived the Norman invasion and persisted in three-quarters of the country until the end of the sixteenth century.

The Irish that was the language of the people at the time of the Norman invasion of 1169 was within a few generations adopted by the foreigners or Gall so that they became 'more Irish than the Irish'. (The Statutes of Kilkenny of 1366 attempted unsuccesfully to prohibit this gaelicisation.) This had always been the pattern: invaders such as the Vikings or more benign 'colonisers' such as the Christianising visitors from Britain at the time of Saint Patrick had been assimilated, superimposing some of their own customs and language but absorbing much of what they found. But with the Tudor reconquest and especially with the successive waves of plantation – Munster, Ulster, Cromwellian – the native Irish were impoverished and made politically powerless, and gradually Irish became the language only of the poor and dispossessed and – most ominously of all – of the illiterate. With the decline of the Gaelic and Old-English aristocracy under the penal laws of the eighteenth century, the hereditary poets and learned men too began to die out. They were the keepers of the flame, the guardians of the learning and lore of the tribe, the scribes and recorders. The loss was incalculable.

When Thomas Davis began writing for the *Nation* in 1842, he calculated that west of the north-south line from Derry to Waterford, Irish was still the first language. The hedge schools, with their strongly classical and Gaelic bent, which were originally meant to counter the penal debarment of Catholics from education and provide the necessary preliminary training for clerical students, continued to exist alongside the parish schools that were permitted by mid-nineteenth century. Irish poetry continued to be written, its early formality gradually being mitigated as it became the voice of the peasant majority. Such poets as Aogán Ó Rathaile, (1675–1729), Cathal Buí Mac Giolla Gunna

(?1680–1755), Seán Clárach Mac Dónaill (1691–1754), Peadar Ó Doirnín (1704–69), Art Mac Cumhaidh (1738–73), Eoghan Rua Ó Súilleabháin (1748–84), Brian Merriman (1749–1803) and many others mourned the loss of greatness and commented upon the condition of the Irish in modes that varied from a satire worthy of the old bards to a modern bawdry. Anonymous songs telling of love, piety and a remarkable zest for life continued to be composed and sung into the middle of the nineteenth century.

Dance, music of harp and pipe, and later of whistle and fiddle, survived all the social deprivation and attempts at obliteration. Some of the parvenu landlords encouraged such itinerant harpists and composers as the great Turlough Carolan (1670–1738) to entertain their guests, reviving a staple feature of Gaelic feasts. The tradition was sufficiently strong throughout the century to permit the organisation of a four-day harp festival in Belfast in 1796 and allow the musical scribe Edward Bunting (1773–1843) to publish three collections of 'ancient' Irish music.

In truth, the extent of the decline of the Irish language from the beginning of the nineteenth century is remarkable and has never been satisfactorily explained. The Great Famine and the subsequent tidal wave of emigration were cataclysmic in their effect, striking as they did primarily at the poorest and therefore monoglot population. With the exception of romantic rebels like Thomas Davis of Young Ireland, Irish political leaders saw no useful purpose for Irish: Daniel O'Connell, though reared in the rich literary and linguistic tradition of south Kerry, was too pragmatic to have time for it. As a Benthamite, practicality was his dominant trait and his acquiscence in the death of the Irish language simply replicated the country's practice. His utilitarian (and Biblical) dismissal was unanswerable: 'A diversity of tongues is no benefit; it was first imposed upon mankind as a curse, at the building of Babel . . . ' Parnell, an aristrocratic landlord from County Wicklow, had no connection with Gaelic Ireland.

The Irish Literary Renaissance is said to date from the final decade of the nineteenth century. The idea that it was generated by a felt need to fill the political vacuum left by the fall of Parnell, and the miserable wrangling that followed, was largely an invention of Yeats, who saw himself as the equivalent literary chief. Perhaps the real reason was the very success of Parnell's political career, the resolution of some of the worst difficulties of the land question and the enlightened policies of the British government who sought to 'kill Home Rule by kindness', i.e. by trying to neutralise nationalist aspirations with social, non-political policies in the 1890s. The last decade of the old century and the first of the new were remarkable in their cultural denseness. They also saw the foundation of Sinn Féin (meaning 'we ourselves') and the Dungannon Clubs. As the name implied, the first was a separatist movement which even had an abstentionist candidate elected in 1908. Its founder was Arthur Griffith (1871–1922), and his approach was as much cultural as political. The advocacy of things Irish and disapproval of all English influences meant that he had strong fraternal links with the Gaelic League (founded in 1893); it also made his movement very sensitive to what it took to be criticism of any aspect of Irish life. He and his followers had no time for such ribald, earthy dramas as Synge's

In the Shadow of the Glen (1903) and *The Playboy of the Western World* (1907). His literary mentor was Thomas Davis and he was able to tolerate any amount of inferior *Nation* poetry if he could advance Davis's recipe for an Irish Ireland.

The Dungannon Clubs were founded by Bulmer Hobson (1883–1969) and Dennis McCullough (1883–1968), both members of the IRB. The name was a gracious nod to the scene of the Ulster Volunteers' 1782 convention. Hobson was a Quaker and, like Griffith, had worked as a printer. His magazine, the *Republic*, which was written by such brilliant (Protestant) journalists as Robert Lynd and James Wilder Good, was remarkably influential in spite of its short life (six months), and takes its place alongside the *Northern Patriot* and the *Shan Van Vocht* run by Alice Milligan and Ethna Carbery (Anna Johnston) as proof that Dublin did not have a monopoly of literary substitutes for parliamentary politics. Like Griffith, Hobson was against the 1916 Rising, believing in a policy of passive resistance and justifying the use of an armed force only for defence. He did his best to prevent the 'action of a small junta within the IRB' and was held incommunicado from the Good Friday until Easter Monday.

The Gaelic League, founded by Douglas Hyde, a Roscommon son of the manse, and Eoin MacNeill, a law clerk from the Antrim Glens, was certainly as significant as the Irish Literary Theatre or the Abbey that was its successor. It was the latest and most successful of a number of initiatives that had begun with the founding of the Royal Irish Academy in 1785. It had as precursors the Ossianic Society of 1853 and most significantly the Society for the Preservation of the Irish Language which was set up by David Comyn, a Protestant from County Clare, in 1876 and which afterwards split to form the Gaelic Union three years later. Hyde had come to notice with a public lecture delivered on November 1892: 'On the necessity for de-Anglicizing the Irish People'. The League was bound to gain the approval of Griffith, as it was explicitly separatist. Davis had advocated a revival of Irish and as a rejection of the imposed language of the colonial masters it was a most potent declaration of revolution. (James Joyce, one of the greatest Irish writers of this amazingly rich period, was moved neither by the League nor the Irish renaissance: he joined a League branch when he was at UCD but left when the teacher, Patrick Pearse found it necessary to denigrate English and adduced one of Joyce's favourite words, 'thunder' as an example of its verbal inadequacy. As the most urban of writers Joyce did not feel much empathy with the Connacht Celtic Twilight.)

The League had twenty years of remarkable success largely because of the high motivation of its original members, its use of the Gaeltacht as a source of the living language and its understanding of the nature of adult education. It was non-sectarian at the start but soon Protestant members were made to feel unwelcome. Hyde himself resigned in 1915 from an organisation which had become dominated by IRB members.

The other association that became prominent at the time had no need to expel Protestants since it was sectarian from its beginning. The Gaelic Athletic Association had been founded in 1884 by Michael Cusack and Maurice Davin and was regarded from 1886 onwards by the

Special Branch as an IRB association – with considerable justification. Even its first patron, Archbishop Thomas Croke, broke with the organisation in 1887 when he found a meeting 'packed to the throat with Fenian leaders.'

After independence, because of the influence of the Gaelic League, all the concomitant parties in the national struggle were committed to the restoration of Irish as the official state language. Cumann na nGaedhal leader W.T. Cosgrave was determined to prove his commitment early. On 1 June 1924 new certificate examinations were set up and it was declared that Irish would be a compulsory subject for the Intermediate Certificate from 1928 and for the Leaving Certificate from 1934. This regulation was in force till 1973, the similar civil service regulation lapsing in 1974. One result of government policy was increased investment in the Gaeltacht areas, partly as reward for their long-preserved linguistic virginity and partly to dam emigration from the areas where Irish was the first language.

Even in the matter of Irish, a narrow and mean-minded (and largely puritanical) clique nearly wrecked the worthy endeavour by its unctuous elitism. These were excoriated by Flann O'Brien in his hilarious squib *An Béal Bocht* (1941), at a time when such satire was much needed. The campaign to restore the use of Irish as a spoken language cannot be said to have been successful. Recent examination results in the subject show a pretty dismal performance, though the increase in numbers of Irish-speaking primary schools and the establishment of both primary and secondary all-Irish schools in Northern Ireland is compensatingly cheering. Many reasonable people have come to cherish Irish for its own sake, to recognise its latent illumination of the Irish psyche and to find a working bilingualism a pleasure and often a convenience.

SELECT BIBLIOGRAPHY

Arthur, P. and Jeffery, K. *Northern Ireland Since 1968*. Oxford, 1988.

Bardon, J. *A History of Ulster*. Belfast, 1992.

Beckett, J. C. *The Making of Modern Ireland 1603–1923*. London, 1966.

Bew, P. *Conflict and Conciliation in Ireland 1890–1910*. Oxford, 1987.

Brown, T. *Ireland: A Social and Cultural History*. London, 1981.

Chadwick, N. *The Celts*. London, 1970.

Clarke, H. B. (ed.). *Irish Cities*. Cork, 1995.

Collins, P. (ed.). *Nationalism and Unionism: Conflict in Ireland 1885–1921*. Belfast, 1994.

Connolly, S. J. (ed.). *The Oxford Companion to Irish History*. Oxford, 1998.

Coogan, T. P. *Ireland Since the Rising*. London, 1966.

————. *The IRA*. London, 1980.

————. *The Troubles*. London, 1995.

de Paor, L. *Divided Ulster*. London, 1970.

Foster, R. F. *Modern Ireland 1600–1972*. London, 1988.

————. *Paddy and Mr Punch*. London, 1993.

————(ed.). *The Oxford History of Ireland*. Oxford, 1989.

Harkness, D. W. *Northern Ireland since 1920*. Dublin, 1983.

Kee, R. *The Green Flag*. London, 1970.

Kinealy, C. *This Great Calamity: Irish Famine, 1845–52*. Dublin, 1994.

Lacy, B., *Siege City, The Story of Derry and Londonderry*. Belfast, 1990.

Lee, J. J. *Ireland 1912–1985, Politics and Society*. Cambridge, 1989.

——.*The Modernisation of Irish Society 1848–1918*. Dublin, 1973.

Litton, H. *The Irish Famine: an Illustrated History*. Dublin, 1994.

Lyons, F. S. L. *Ireland since the Famine*. London, 1971.

————-. *Charles Stewart Parnell*. London, 1977.

McCann, E. *War and an Irish Town*. London, 1974.

Moody, T. W. and Martin, F. X. (eds.). *The Course of Irish History*. Cork, 1994.

Ó Broin, A. *Beyond the Black Pig's Dyke*. Cork, 1995.

O'Connor, F. *In Search of a State*. Belfast, 1993.

O'Faolain, S. *King of the Beggars*. London, 1938.

————. *The Great O'Neill*. London, 1942.

————. *The Irish*. London, 1947.

Ó Gráda, C. *The Great Irish Famine*. Cambridge, 1995.

Póirtéir, C. (ed.). *The Great Irish Famine*. Cork, 1995.

Raftery, J. et al. *The Celts*. Cork, 1964.

Stewart, A. T. Q. *The Ulster Crisis*. London, 1967.

Walker, B. *Ulster Politics: The Formative Years 1869–86*. Belfast 1989.

Whyte, J. *Church and State in Modern Ireland 1923–1979*. London, 1980.